CONTENT

Content Development by Demetra Georgopoulos
Illustration and Design by Mike Polito

Phonics: Beginning Sounds

Pre K - Kindergarten

Designed to reinforce essential reading skills!

By completing this workbook, your child will gain systematic practice in the following concepts:

- Identifying letters A - Z
- Printing letters A - Z
- Reading colour words
- Identifying consonant sounds
- Identifying short and long vowel sounds

Colour in this picture.

We acknowledge the financial support of the Government of Canada through the Canada Book Fund for our publishing activities.

Government of Canada   Gouvernement du Canada   Canada

Trace and read the colours.

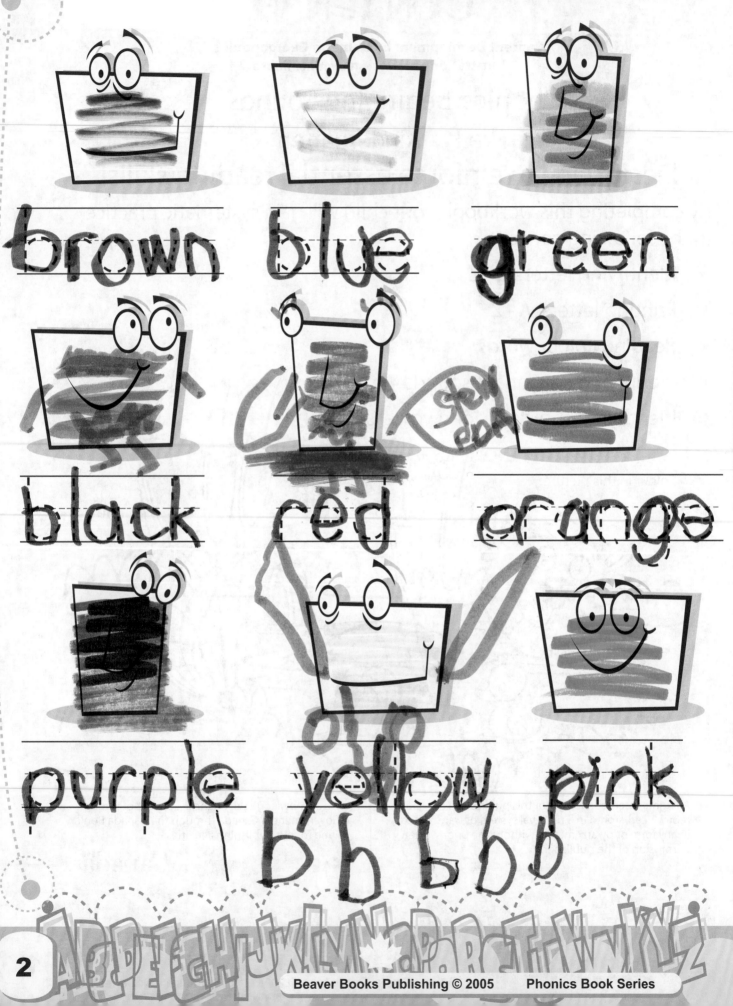

brown   blue   green

black   red   orange

purple   yellow   pink

Consonant Sounds: Letter Bb

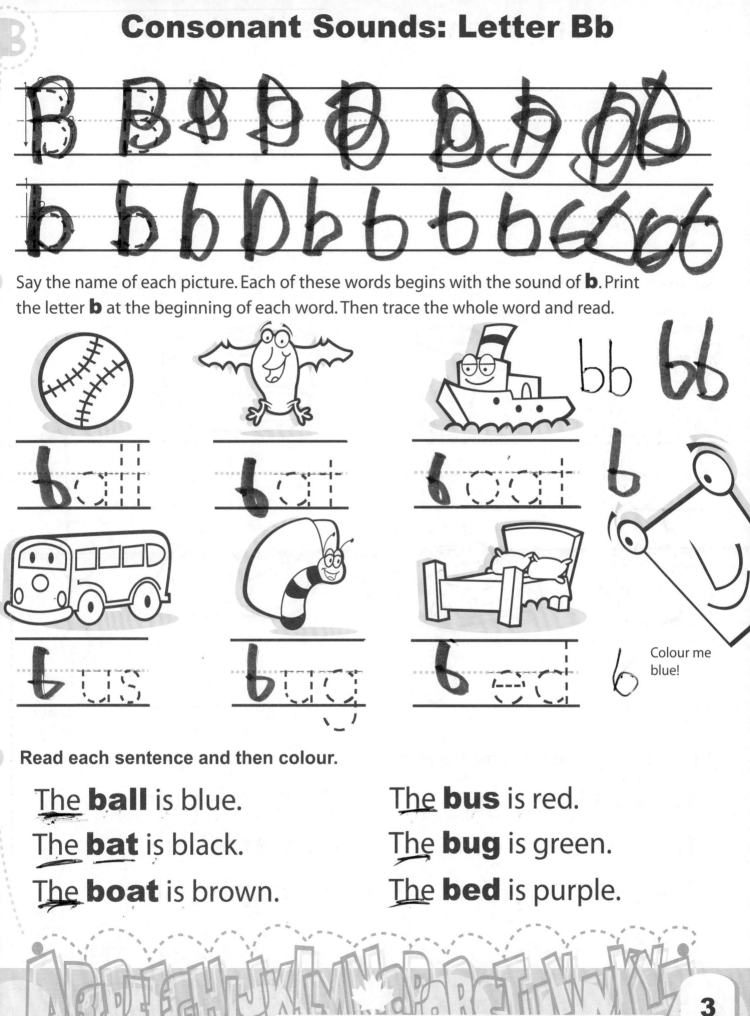

Say the name of each picture. Each of these words begins with the sound of **b**. Print the letter **b** at the beginning of each word. Then trace the whole word and read.

bb

Colour me blue!

ball bat boat

bus bug bed

Read each sentence and then colour.

The **ball** is blue.

The **bat** is black.

The **boat** is brown.

The **bus** is red.

The **bug** is green.

The **bed** is purple.

Beaver Books Publishing © 2005   Phonics Book Series

Consonant Sounds: Letter Cc

Say the name of each picture. Each of these words begins with the sound of **c**. Print the letter **c** at the beginning of each word. Then trace the whole word and read.

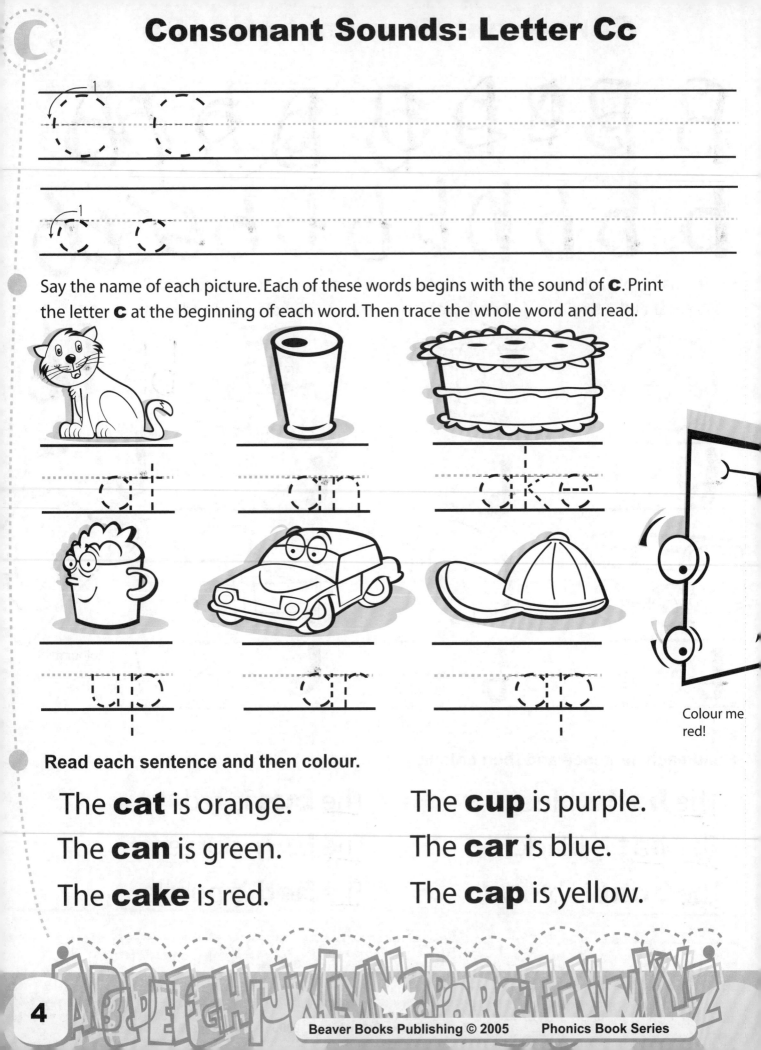

at

an

ake

up

ar

ap

Colour me red!

Read each sentence and then colour.

The **cat** is orange.

The **can** is green.

The **cake** is red.

The **cup** is purple.

The **car** is blue.

The **cap** is yellow.

Beaver Books Publishing © 2005   Phonics Book Series

Consonant Sounds: Letter Dd

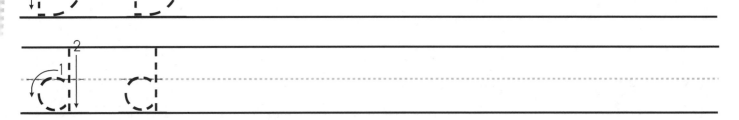

Say the name of each picture. Each of these words begins with the sound of **d**. Print the letter **d** at the beginning of each word. Then trace the whole word and read.

Colour me yellow!

Read each sentence and then colour.

The **dog** is brown.

The **door** is yellow.

The **duck** is orange.

The **dress** is pink.

The **dot** is black.

The **doll** is purple.

Beaver Books Publishing © 2005   Phonics Book Series

Consonant Sounds: Letter Ss

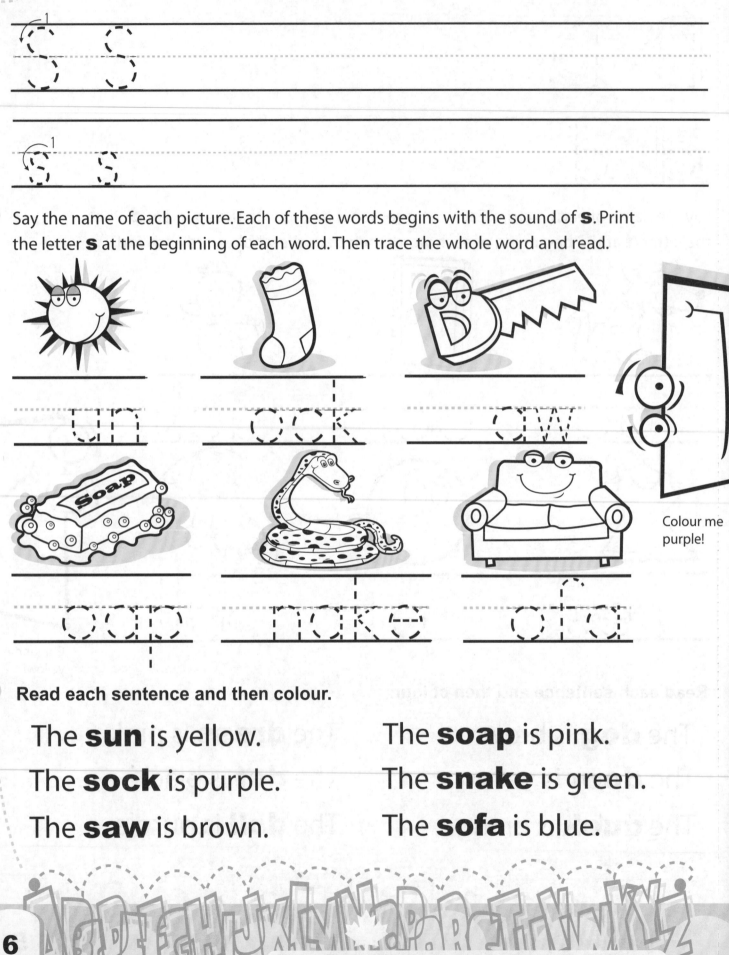

Say the name of each picture. Each of these words begins with the sound of **s**. Print the letter **s** at the beginning of each word. Then trace the whole word and read.

_un   _ock   _aw

Colour me purple!

_oap   _nake   _ofa

Read each sentence and then colour.

The **sun** is yellow.   The **soap** is pink.

The **sock** is purple.   The **snake** is green.

The **saw** is brown.   The **sofa** is blue.

Beaver Books Publishing © 2005   Phonics Book Series

Consonant Sounds: Letter Tt

Say the name of each picture. Each of these words begins with the sound of **t**. Print the letter **t** at the beginning of each word. Then trace the whole word and read.

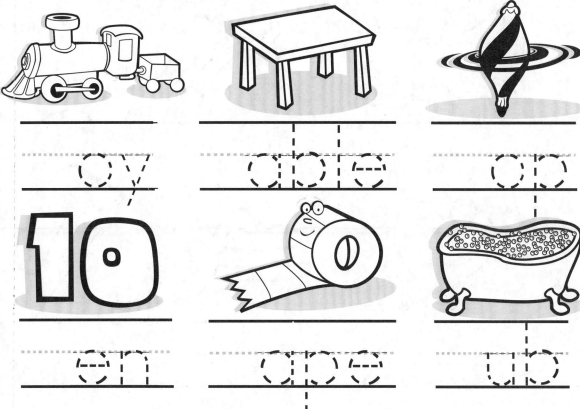

Colour me orange!

Read each sentence and then colour.

The **toy** is pink.

The **table** is blue.

The **top** is green.

The **ten** is red.

The **tape** is orange.

The **tub** is yellow.

Beaver Books Publishing © 2005   Phonics Book Series

Consonant Sounds: Letter Hh

Say the name of each picture. Each of these words begins with the sound of **h**. Print the letter **h** at the beginning of each word. Then trace the whole word and read.

Colour me green!

Read each sentence and then colour.

The **hat** is pink.

The **hen** is red.

The **hand** is orange.

The **heart** is yellow.

The **hill** is brown.

The **hose** is green.

Beaver Books Publishing © 2005   Phonics Book Series

Consonant Sounds: Letter Mm

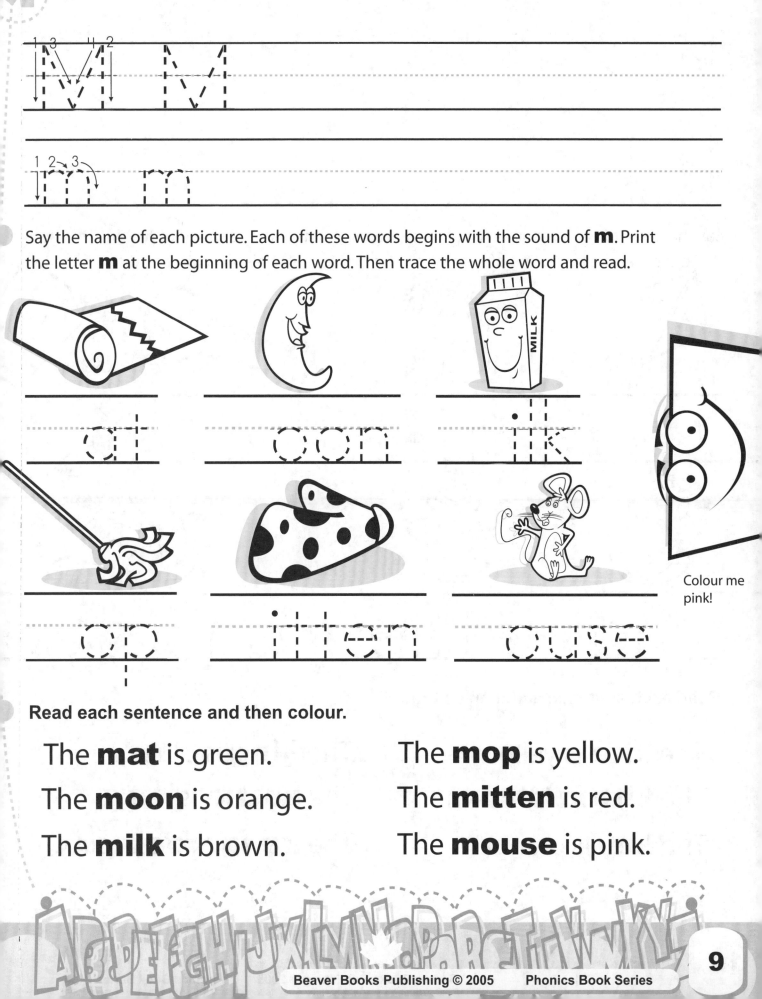

M M

m m

Say the name of each picture. Each of these words begins with the sound of **m**. Print the letter **m** at the beginning of each word. Then trace the whole word and read.

at   oon   ilk

Colour me pink!

op   itten   ouse

Read each sentence and then colour.

The **mat** is green.   The **mop** is yellow.

The **moon** is orange.   The **mitten** is red.

The **milk** is brown.   The **mouse** is pink.

Consonant Sounds: Letter Kk

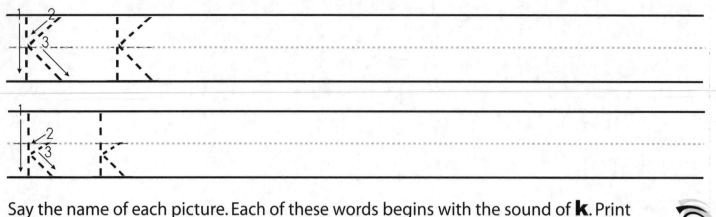

Say the name of each picture. Each of these words begins with the sound of **k**. Print the letter **k** at the beginning of each word. Then trace the whole word and read.

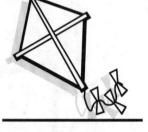  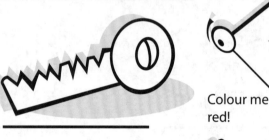

Colour me red!

_ite _itten _ey

_ing _ettle _angaroo

Read each sentence and then colour.

The **kite** is yellow.

The **kitten** is brown.

The **key** is orange.

The **king** is blue.

The **kettle** is red.

The **kangaroo** is pink.

Beaver Books Publishing © 2005   Phonics Book Series

Consonant Sounds: Letter Jj

J J

j j

Say the name of each picture. Each of these words begins with the sound of **j**. Print the letter **j** at the beginning of each word. Then trace the whole word and read.

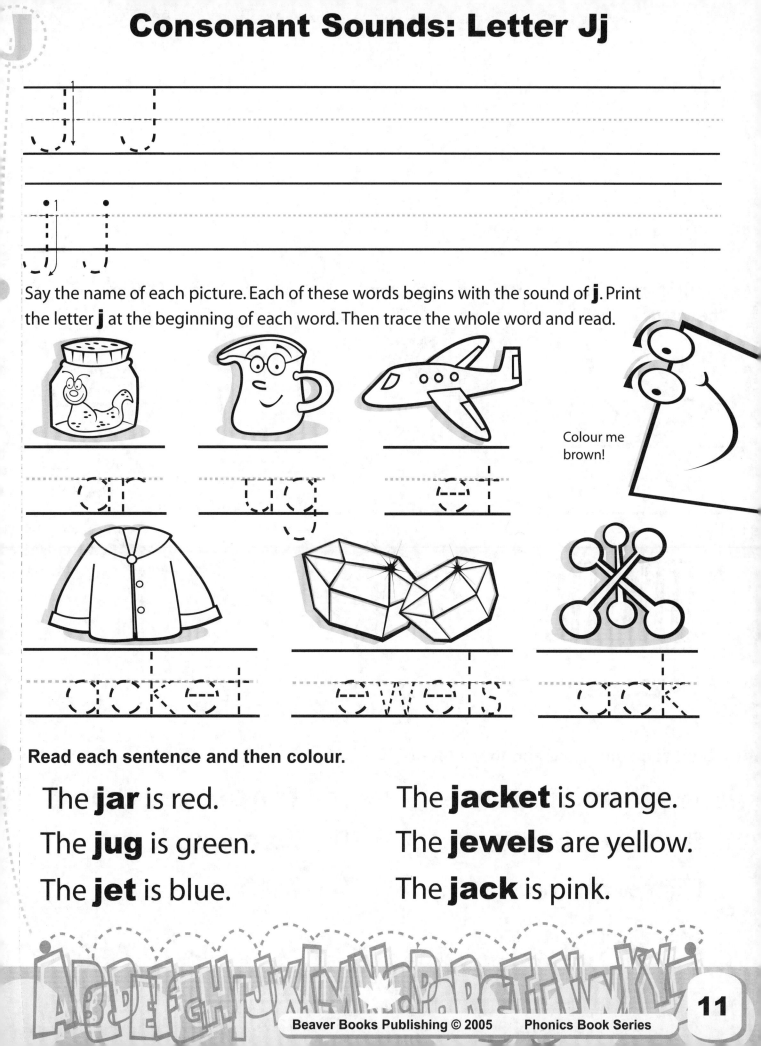

ar   ug   et

Colour me brown!

acket   ewels   ack

Read each sentence and then colour.

The **jar** is red.

The **jug** is green.

The **jet** is blue.

The **jacket** is orange.

The **jewels** are yellow.

The **jack** is pink.

Beaver Books Publishing © 2005   Phonics Book Series

Consonant Sounds: Letter Ff

Say the name of each picture. Each of these words begins with the sound of **f**. Print the letter **f** at the beginning of each word. Then trace the whole word and read.

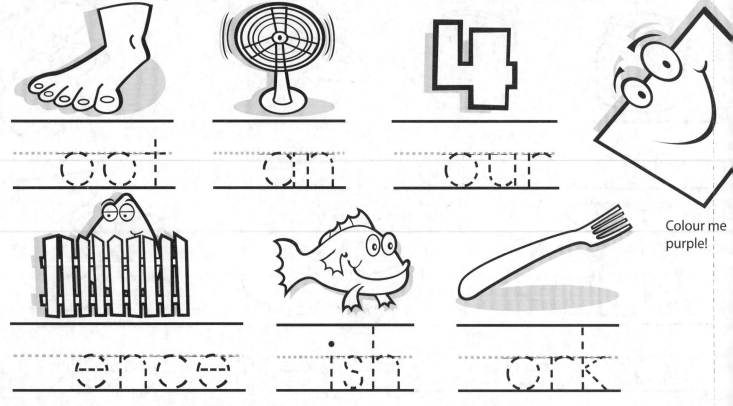

Colour me purple!

Read each sentence and then colour.

The **foot** is brown.

The **fan** is blue.

The **four** is red.

The **fence** is black.

The **fish** is pink.

The **fork** is green.

Beaver Books Publishing © 2005   Phonics Book Series

Consonant Sounds: Letter Gg

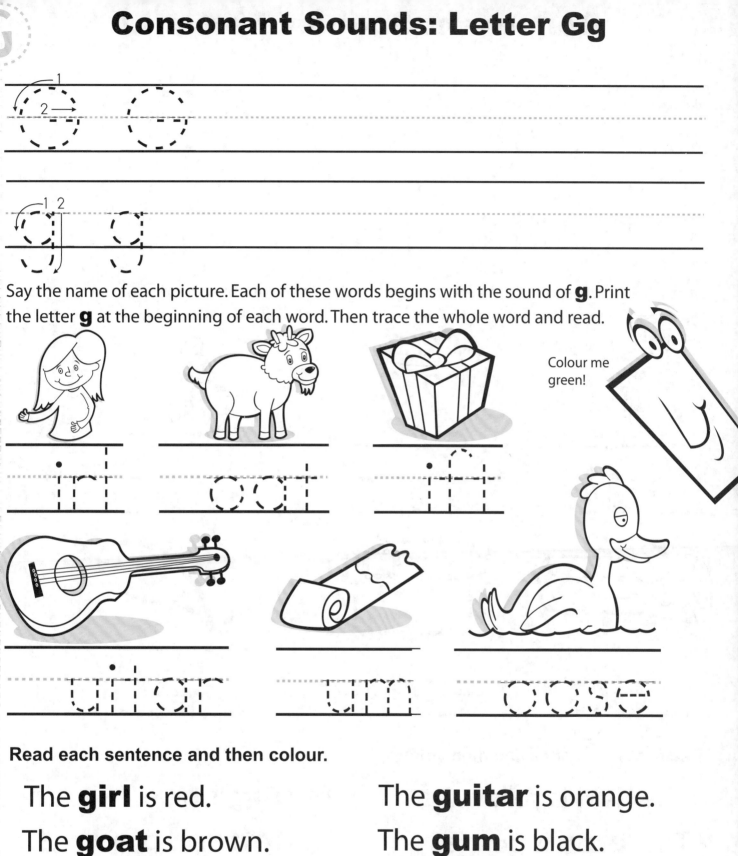

Say the name of each picture. Each of these words begins with the sound of **g**. Print the letter **g** at the beginning of each word. Then trace the whole word and read.

Colour me green!

in   oat   ift

uitar   um   oose

Read each sentence and then colour.

The **girl** is red.

The **goat** is brown.

The **gift** is blue.

The **guitar** is orange.

The **gum** is black.

The **goose** is yellow.

Consonant Sounds: Letter Ll

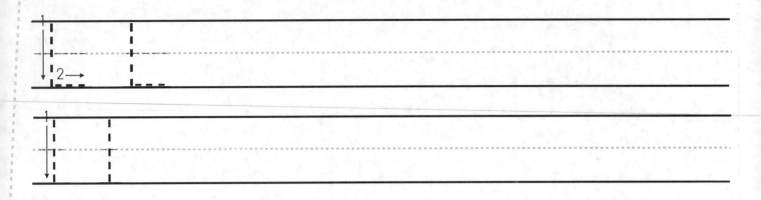

Say the name of each picture. Each of these words begins with the sound of **l**. Print the letter **l** at the beginning of each word. Then trace the whole word and read.

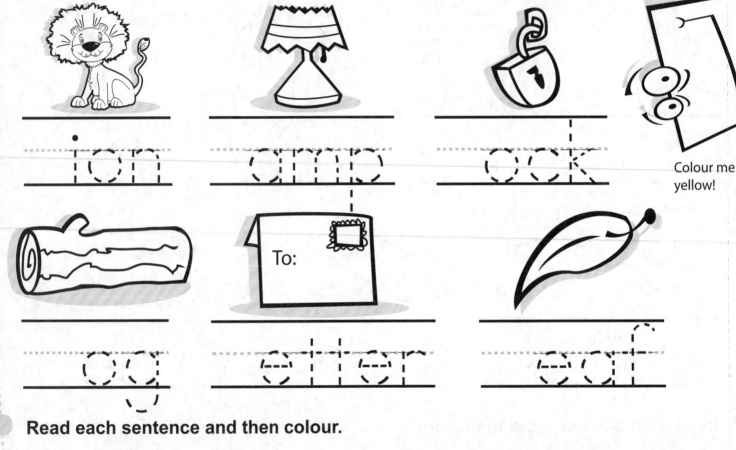

Colour me yellow!

Read each sentence and then colour.

The **lion** is yellow.

The **lamp** is purple.

The **lock** is brown.

The **log** is blue.

The **letter** is pink.

The **leaf** is green.

Beaver Books Publishing © 2005   **Phonics Book Series**

Consonant Sounds: Letter Nn

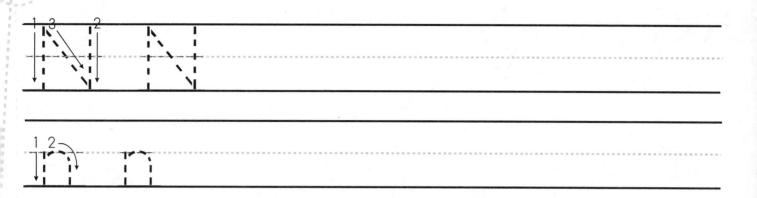

Say the name of each picture. Each of these words begins with the sound of **n**. Print the letter **n** at the beginning of each word. Then trace the whole word and read.

Colour me green!

Read each sentence and then colour.

The **net** is yellow.

The **nest** is purple.

The **nut** is brown.

The **nail** is blue.

The **nose** is pink.

The **nine** is green.

Beaver Books Publishing © 2005   Phonics Book Series

Consonant Sounds: Letter Ww

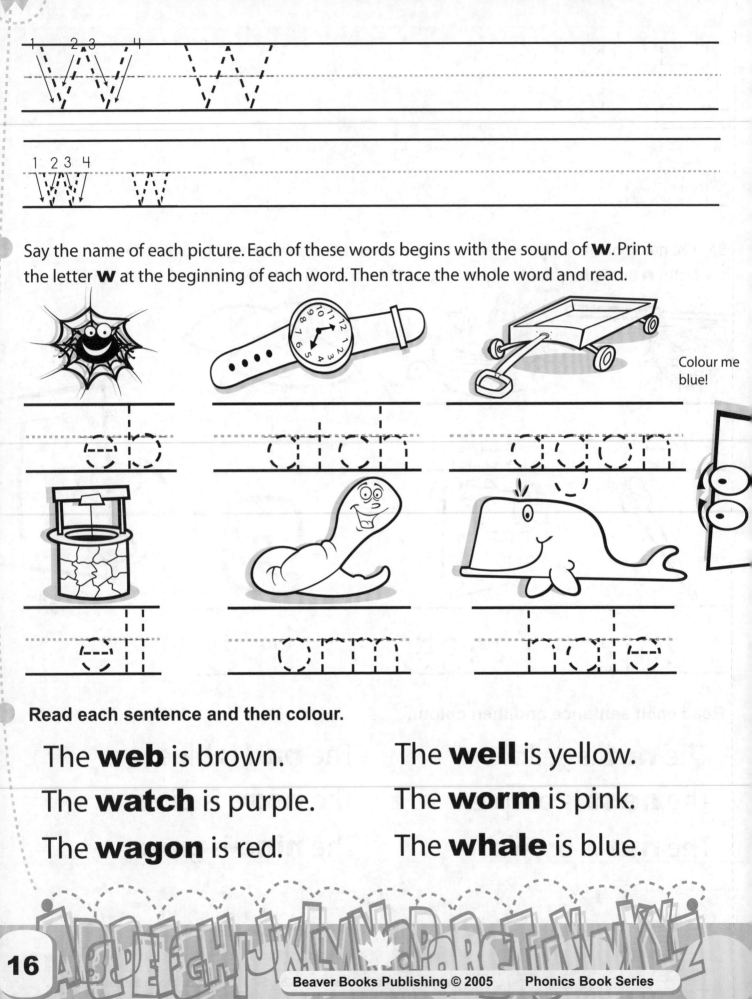

Say the name of each picture. Each of these words begins with the sound of **w**. Print the letter **w** at the beginning of each word. Then trace the whole word and read.

Colour me blue!

Read each sentence and then colour.

The **web** is brown.

The **watch** is purple.

The **wagon** is red.

The **well** is yellow.

The **worm** is pink.

The **whale** is blue.

Beaver Books Publishing © 2005   Phonics Book Series

Consonant Sounds: Letter Rr

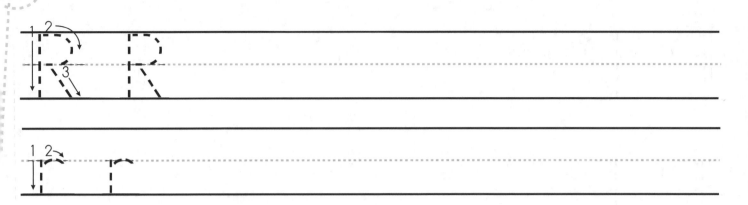

Say the name of each picture. Each of these words begins with the sound of **r**. Print the letter **r** at the beginning of each word. Then trace the whole word and read.

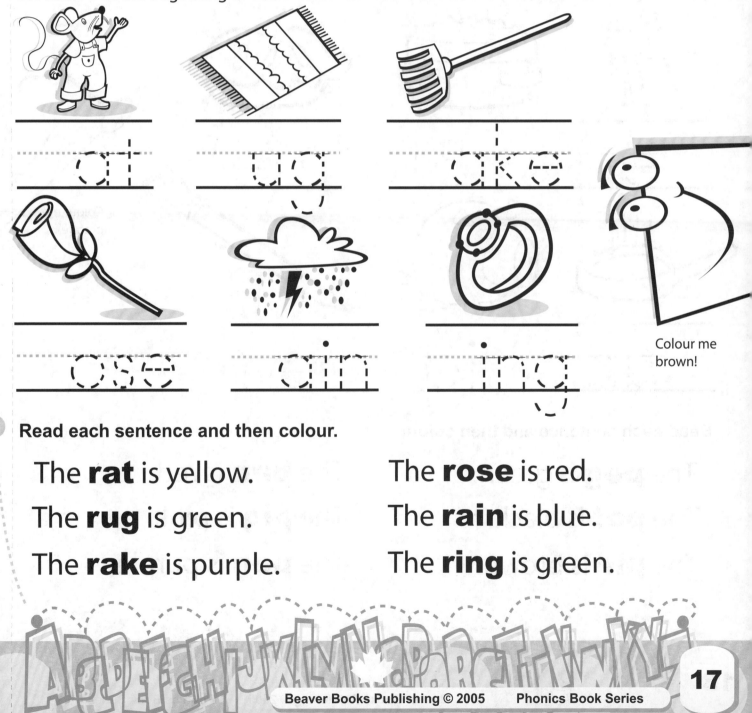

Colour me brown!

Read each sentence and then colour.

The **rat** is yellow.

The **rug** is green.

The **rake** is purple.

The **rose** is red.

The **rain** is blue.

The **ring** is green.

Beaver Books Publishing © 2005   Phonics Book Series

Consonant Sounds: Letter Pp

Say the name of each picture. Each of these words begins with the sound of **p**. Print the letter **p** at the beginning of each word. Then trace the whole word and read.

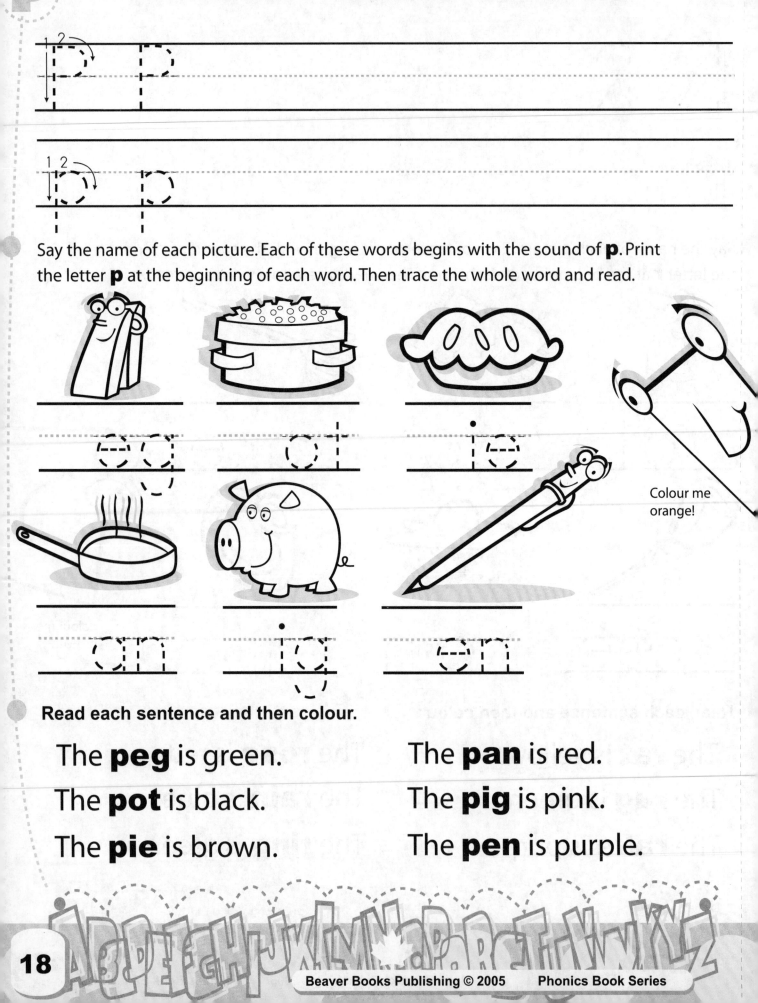

Colour me orange!

Read each sentence and then colour.

The **peg** is green.

The **pot** is black.

The **pie** is brown.

The **pan** is red.

The **pig** is pink.

The **pen** is purple.

Beaver Books Publishing © 2005   Phonics Book Series

Consonant Sounds: Letter Qq

Say the name of each picture. Each of these words begins with the sound of **q**. Print the letter **q** at the beginning of each word. Then trace the whole word and read.

queen

quail

quilt

quill

Colour me pink!

Read each sentence and then colour.

The **queen** is blue.

The **quail** is brown.

The **quilt** is red.

The **quill** is yellow.

Beaver Books Publishing © 2005   Phonics Book Series

Consonant Sounds: Letter Vv

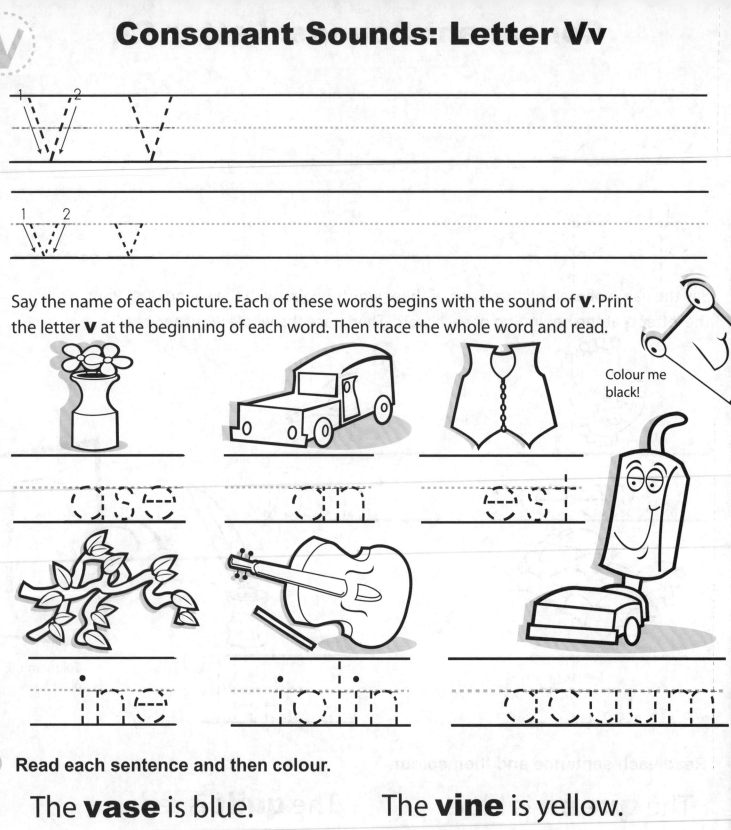

Say the name of each picture. Each of these words begins with the sound of **v**. Print the letter **v** at the beginning of each word. Then trace the whole word and read.

Colour me black!

ase   an   est

ine   iolin   acuum

Read each sentence and then colour.

The **vase** is blue.   The **vine** is yellow.

The **van** is green.   The **violin** is brown.

The **vest** is red.   The **vacuum** is red.

Beaver Books Publishing © 2005   Phonics Book Series

Consonant Sounds: Letter Xx

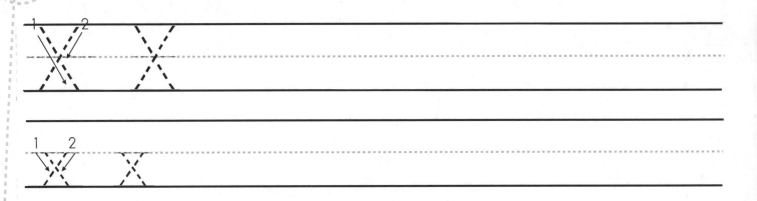

Say the name of each picture. Each of these words begins with the sound of **x**. Print the letter **x** at the beginning of each word. Then trace the whole word and read.

‐ray

xylophone

Read each sentence and then colour.

The **x-ray** is blue.

The **xylophone** is brown.

Colour me red!

Beaver Books Publishing © 2005   Phonics Book Series

Consonant Sounds: Letter Yy

Y Y Y

Y Y

Say the name of each picture. Each of these words begins with the sound of **y**. Print the letter **y** at the beginning of each word. Then trace the whole word and read.

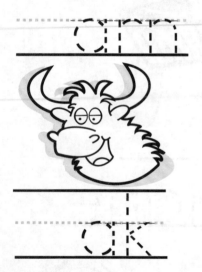

arn

o-yo

ak

olk

Colour me blue!

Read each sentence and then colour.

The **yarn** is blue.

The **yo-yo** is brown.

The **yak** is yellow.

The **yolk** is orange.

Consonant Sounds: Letter Zz

Say the name of each picture. Each of these words begins with the sound of **z**. Print the letter **z** at the beginning of each word. Then trace the whole word and read.

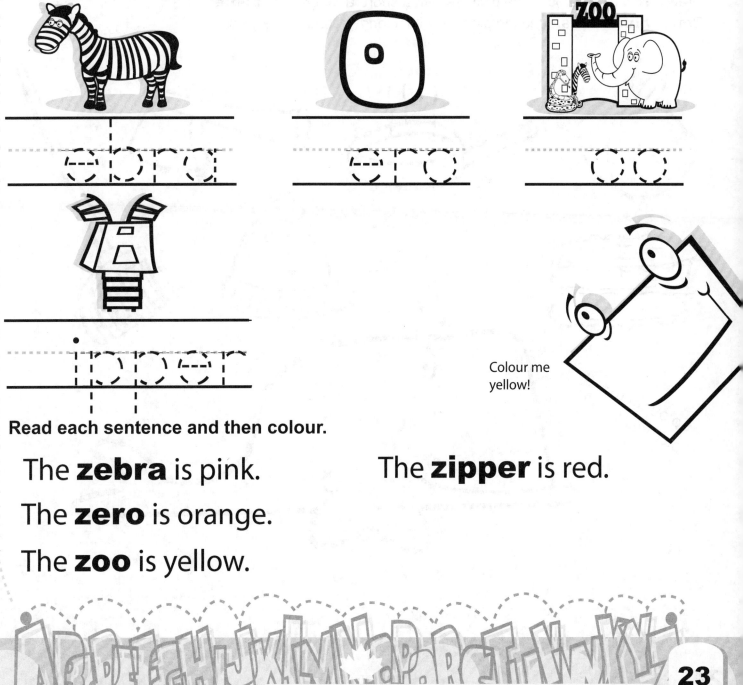

Colour me yellow!

Read each sentence and then colour.

The **zebra** is pink.

The **zero** is orange.

The **zoo** is yellow.

The **zipper** is red.

Beaver Books Publishing © 2005   Phonics Book Series

Vowel Sounds: Letter Aa

Long "a" and short "a"

Draw a **red** circle around the pictures with a short "a" sound like **apple**.

Draw a **blue** circle around the pictures with a long "a" sound like **pan**.

Colour in the pictures!

Vowel Sounds: Letter Ee

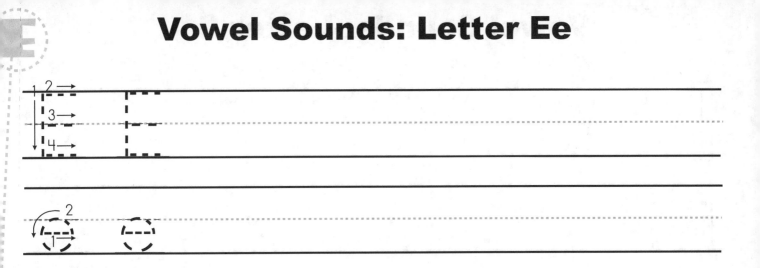

Long "e" and short "e"

Draw a **red** circle around the pictures with a short "e" sound like **egg**.
Draw a **blue** circle around the pictures with a long "e" sound like **tree**.

Colour in the pictures!

Beaver Books Publishing © 2005   **Phonics Book Series**

Vowel Sounds: Letter Ii

Long "i" and short "i"

Draw a **red** circle around the pictures with a short "i" sound like **fish**.

Draw a **blue** circle around the pictures with a long "i" sound like **fire**.

Colour in the pictures!

Vowel Sounds: Letter Oo

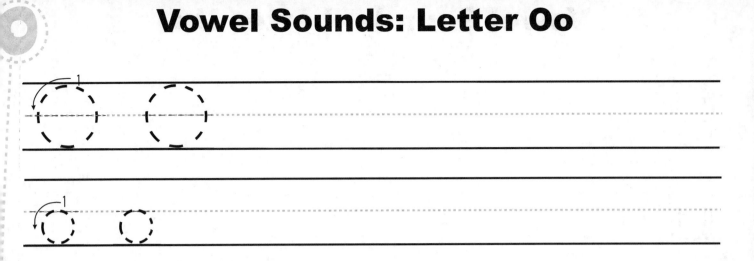

Long "o" and short "o"

Draw a **red** circle around the pictures with a short "o" sound like **pot**.
Draw a **blue** circle around the pictures with a long "o" sound like **bone**.

Colour in the pictures!

Beaver Books Publishing © 2005   Phonics Book Series

Vowel Sounds: Letter Uu

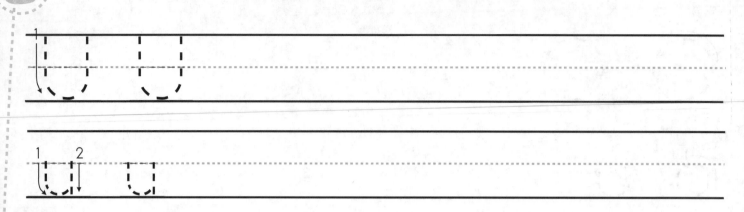

Long "u" and short "u"

Draw a **red** circle around the pictures with a short "u" sound like **jug**.
Draw a **blue** circle around the pictures with a long "u" sound like **cube**.

Colour in the pictures!

Beaver Books Publishing © 2005   Phonics Book Series

Sounding it out!

Say the name of each picture. Print the letter at the beginning of each word.
Then trace the whole word and read.

_ _ _ _ _ _ _ _ _ _ _ _
og   uail   an

atoo   etter   iolin

ak   ak   uill

og   ot   et

Sounding it out!

Say the name of each picture. Print the letter at the beginning of each word.
Then trace the whole word and read.

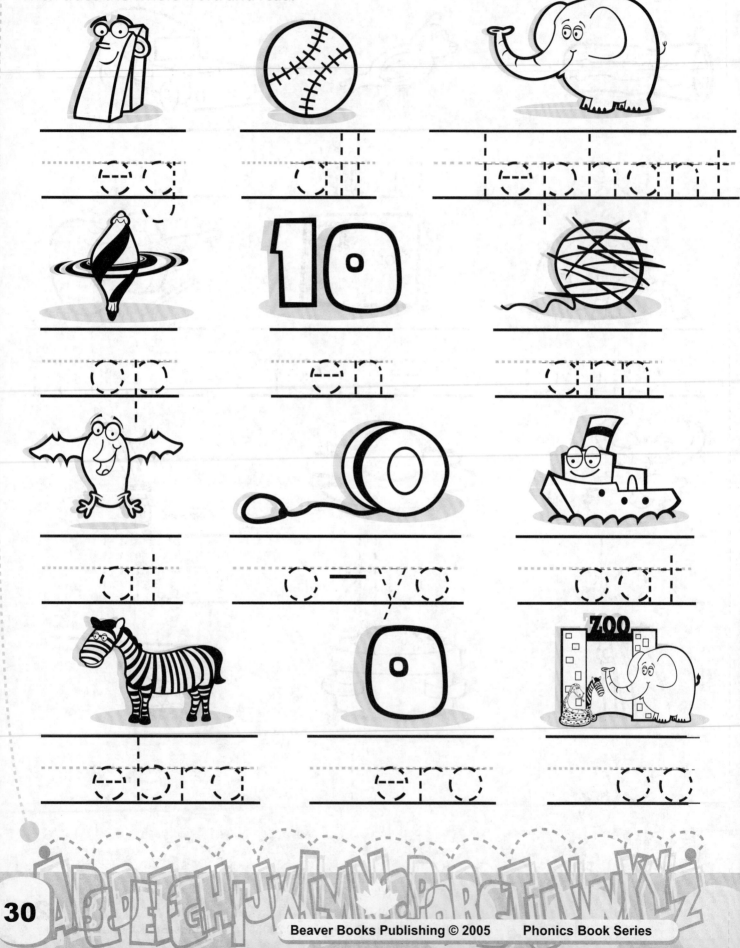

Beaver Books Publishing © 2005   Phonics Book Series

Sounding it out!

Say the name of each picture. Print the letter at the beginning of each word.
Then trace the whole word and read.

ueen

an

ake

uilt

oot

an

ug

ake

ouse

all

xe

etter

Sounding it out!

Say the name of each picture. Print the letter at the beginning of each word.
Then trace the whole word and read.

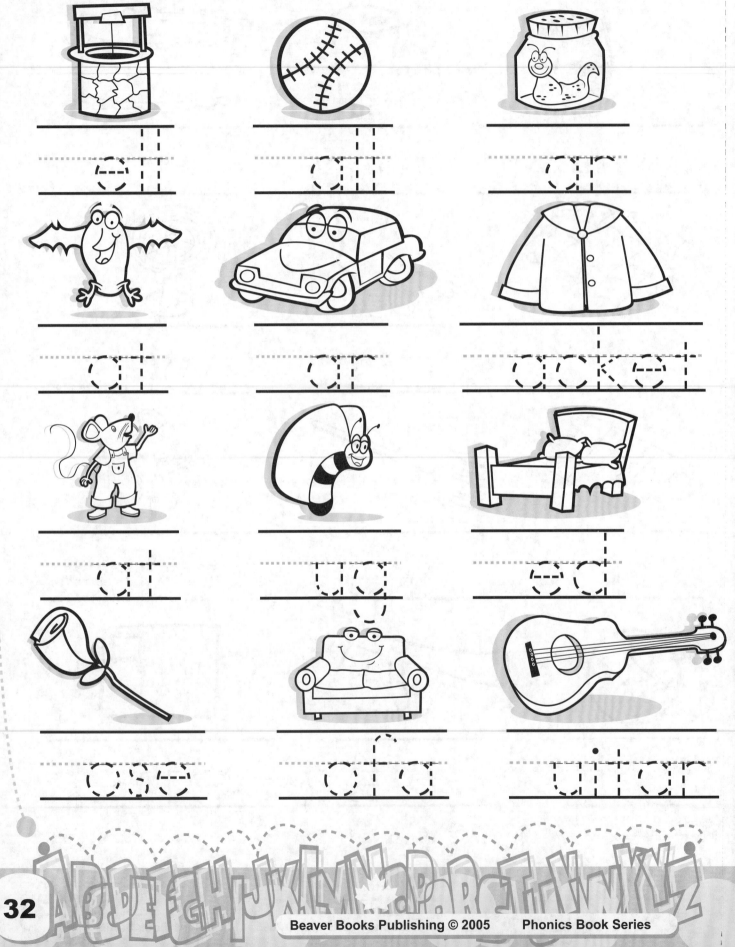

Beaver Books Publishing © 2005   Phonics Book Series

Sounding it out!

Say the name of each picture. Print the letter at the beginning of each word.
Then trace the whole word and read.

Beaver Books Publishing © 2005   Phonics Book Series

Sounding it out!

Say the name of each picture. Print the letter at the beginning of each word. Then trace the whole word and read.

ebra   ock   ero

ipper   ape   at

ain   ing   ose

atch   agon   eb

Sounding it out!

Say the name of each picture. Print the letter at the beginning of each word. Then trace the whole word and read.

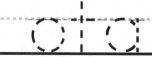

_____ ase

_____ an

_____ acuum

_____ est

_____ iolin

_____ ine

_____ un

_____ ock

_____ aw

_____ oap

_____ nake

_____ ofa

Beaver Books Publishing © 2005   **Phonics Book Series**

Sounding it out!

Say the name of each picture. Print the letter at the beginning of each word.
Then trace the whole word and read.

Beaver Books Publishing © 2005   Phonics Book Series

Sounding it out!

Say the name of each picture. Print the letter at the beginning of each word.
Then trace the whole word and read.

_at_   _ug_   _ake_

ose   _ain_   _ing_

_eb_   _atch_   _agon_

ell   _orm_   _hale_

Sounding it out!

Say the name of each picture. Print the letter at the beginning of each word.
Then trace the whole word and read.

___ion

___amp

___ock

___og

___etter

___eaf

___oot

___an

___our

___ence

___ish

___ork

Sounding it out!

Say the name of each picture. Print the letter at the beginning of each word.
Then trace the whole word and read.

_ar

_ug

_et

_acket

_ewels

_ack

_in

_oat

_if

_uitar

_um

_oose

Sounding it out!

Say the name of each picture. Print the letter at the beginning of each word. Then trace the whole word and read.

ite   itten   ey

ing   ix   even

ar   ug   et

at   an   ake

Beaver Books Publishing © 2005   Phonics Book Series

Sounding it out!

Say the name of each picture. Print the letter at the beginning of each word.
Then trace the whole word and read.

Sounding it out!

Say the name of each picture. Print the letter at the beginning of each word.
Then trace the whole word and read.

____   un

____   ock

____   aw

____   en

____   ape

____   ub

____   us

____   ug

____   ed

____   ueen

____   uail

____   uill

Beaver Books Publishing © 2005   Phonics Book Series

Sounding it out!

Say the name of each picture. Print the letter at the beginning of each word.
Then trace the whole word and read.

_____ og

_____ oor

_____ uck

_____ ress

_____ ot

_____ oll

_____ ag

_____ ock

_____ ipper

_____ ray

_____ lephant

Beaver Books Publishing © 2005   **Phonics Book Series**

BEAVER BOOKS

Certificate of Completion

Great work!

Name: _____

You are fantastic!

Phonics Book Series